W9-BXZ-372

I didn't know that

chimps
use
tools

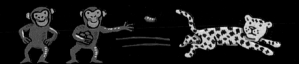

© Aladdin Books Ltd 1999
Produced by
Aladdin Books Ltd
28 Percy Street
London W1P 0LD

First published in the United States in 1999 by
Copper Beech Books,
an imprint of
The Millbrook Press
2 Old New Milford Road
Brookfield, Connecticut 06804

Concept, editorial and design by
David West Children's Books

Designer: Robert Perry

Illustrators: Chris Shields – Wildlife Art Agency Ltd.,
Jo Moore

Printed in Belgium
5 4 3 2 1

Cataloging-in-Publication data is on file at the
Library of Congress.

ISBN 0-7613-0874-1 (lib.bdg.)
ISBN 0-7613-0786-9 (trade hardcover)

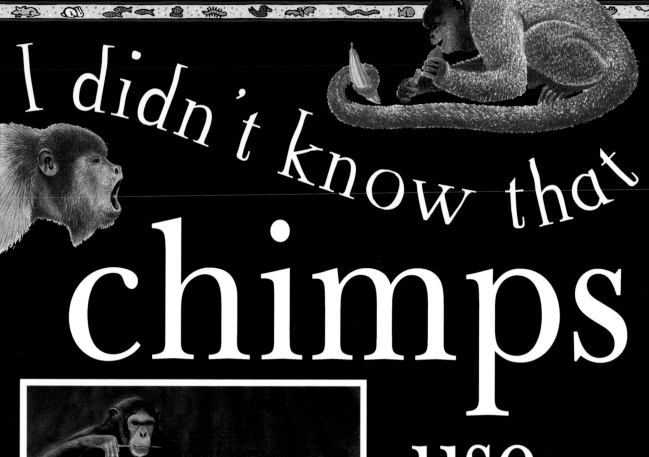

I didn't know that

chimps

use

tools

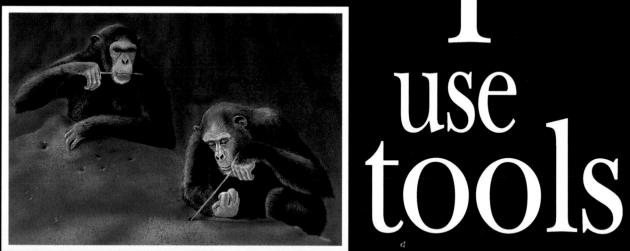

Claire Llewellyn

COPPER BEECH BOOKS
BROOKFIELD, CONNECTICUT

I didn't know that

apes are different from monkeys 6

some monkeys live in the mountains 9

some monkeys have three hands 11

gibbons are acrobats 12

some monkeys live in large groups 14

some monkeys wear makeup 17

primates make wonderful parents 18

chimps use tools 20

eagles kill monkeys 22

some gorillas have silver fur 24

some monkeys and apes are orphans 27

a monkey is the noisiest land animal 29

glossary 30

index 32

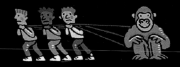

Introduction

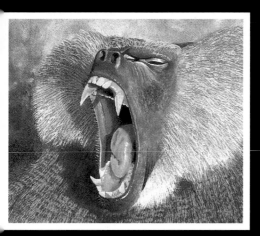

Did *you* know that some monkeys have fangs? ... that howler monkeys are the loudest land animals? ... that macaques wash their food? ... that a gorilla has learned sign language?

Discover for yourself amazing facts about monkeys and apes – their differences, what they eat, how they communicate and show friendship, how they have babies, who their enemies are, and more.

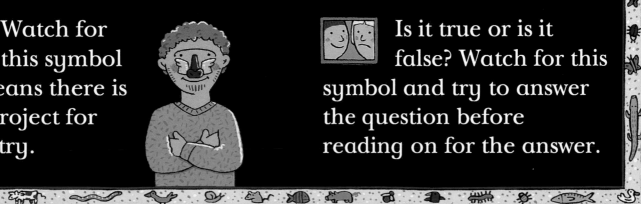

Watch for this symbol that means there is a fun project for you to try.

Is it true or is it false? Watch for this symbol and try to answer the question before reading on for the answer.

forget t

I didn't know that

apes are different from monkeys. They are larger and can stand upright on their back feet. Apes include orangutans, chimpanzees, gorillas, and gibbons. Apes do not have monkeys' useful tails.

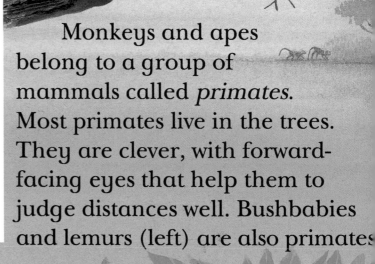

SEARCH & FIND

Can you find four monkeys and two apes?

Mangabey

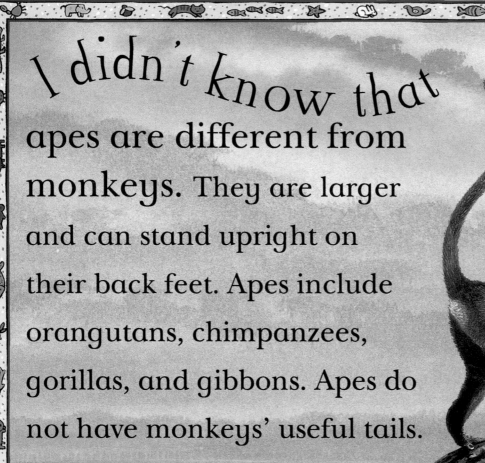

Monkeys and apes belong to a group of mammals called *primates*. Most primates live in the trees. They are clever, with forward-facing eyes that help them to judge distances well. Bushbabies and lemurs (left) are also primates.

Lowland gorilla

True or false?
Humans are primates.

Answer: **True**
Humans belong to the same family as apes and monkeys, but are not directly related. Scientists who study ancient *fossils* think that humans and apes shared a common *ancestor* about 10 million years ago.

Apes have faces that are almost human.

There are no apes in South America.

African and Asian monkeys, like the colobus monkey, have downward-pointing nostrils and *sitting pads* on their bottom. South American monkeys, such as capuchins, have sideways-facing nostrils and no sitting pads.

Capuchin

Colobus

Not all apes and monkeys live in forests. Some African and Asian monkeys live in muddy swamps. Baboons (below) prefer grasslands or dry, rocky hills.

8

Japanese macaque

I didn't know that

some monkeys live in the mountains. Japanese macaques live in the mountains of northern Japan. In winter, they like to sit in hot springs that bubble up from under the ground. It's a great winter warm-up!

True or false?
No monkeys live in Europe.

Answer: **False**
Barbary apes live on the Rock of Gibraltar, south of Spain. They were probably brought over from Africa many years ago.

The monkeys of South America live entirely in the trees.

True or false?
Some apes eat meat.

Answer: **True**
As well as eating fruit, chimpanzees like the taste of meat. They are clever hunters, and may work together to catch colobus monkeys, antelopes, or pigs – but there is fierce competition for the meat when the prey is caught.

Woolly monkey

The marmosets of South America use their long, sharp teeth to make holes in trees, and suck the sweet, sticky *sap* (left).

Pygmy marmoset

Monkeys feed on fruit in the forest, and are very useful for spreading seeds. A small group of monkeys can "plant" thousands of seeds every day.

Spider monkey

I didn't know that

some monkeys have three hands. The spider and woolly monkeys of South America use their long, strong tail as an extra arm. The tail is *prehensile*, which means it can curl around a branch and hold on tight.

! Animals that eat lots of leaves usually have potbellies.

Hang from a gymnasium bar for a while and you'll see why gibbons need long, hooked fingers and strong muscles in their arms!

I didn't know that

gibbons are acrobats.

Gibbons are at home in the forests of Asia. They have very long arms and swing easily from tree to tree, moving one arm over the other. This is called *brachiating*.

Lar gibbon

Gibbons probably move through the forest faster than any other animal.

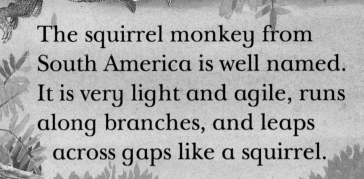

The squirrel monkey from South America is well named. It is very light and agile, runs along branches, and leaps across gaps like a squirrel.

SEARCH & FIND SEARCH & FIND

Can you find five butterflies?

Gorillas and chimpanzees walk on the knuckles of their hands and the soles of their feet. This is known as knuckle-walking.

I didn't know that

some monkeys live in large groups. Baboons live on open grasslands in large groups called troops. Males lead the troops and take turns acting as guards on the lookout for cheetahs and lions.

Apes and monkeys groom one another. It creates a bond between group members, and helps to keep them all friendly. It also keeps them clean!

SEARCH & FIND
Can you find the hiding lion?
FIND & SEARCH

In a group of chimpanzees, the biggest, oldest, and cleverest chimps become more important than the others. Male chimps often threaten each other to try and improve their ranking.

 True or false?
Some apes live all alone.

Answer: **True**

Orangutans live deep in the rain forests of Southeast Asia. Each animal stays in its own part of the forest, well away from its neighbors. The females live in small family groups with just a baby or two.

Savanna baboons

Gibbons live in small groups, just mom, dad, and the kids.

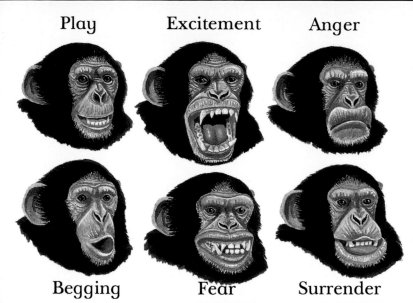

Play   Excitement   Anger

Begging   Fear   Surrender

Chimpanzees make all sorts of faces, and can also make many different sounds. This helps them to keep in touch with each other, avoid arguments, and warn one another of danger.

 True or false?
A female monkey blushes with her bottom.

Answer: **True**
From time to time, a female monkey's sitting pads become large and bright pink. This is a clear signal to the males that she is ready to mate.

Apes' and monkeys' faces are bare to show their *expressions.*

Mandrill

I didn't know that

some monkeys wear makeup. Mandrills live in the African rain forest. The male's brightly-colored face shows up well in the forest and helps him to attract a mate.

Turn yourself into a handsome mandrill. Find a set of face paints and a mirror and copy the monkey's markings. Draw the outline of the design before you color it in.

SEARCH & FIND & SEARCH & FIND

Can you find the python?

I didn't know that primates make wonderful parents. Most apes and monkeys have one baby at a time and give it lots of love. A mother teaches her baby all it needs to know and protects it for years.

Baby chimpanzees play for hours. They learn to swing and climb through the trees and to behave properly with the other chimps in the group.

Chimpanzee

True or false?
The mother always looks after a new baby.

Answer: **False**
A male titi is a loving father (below). He carries the baby around with him everywhere and only hands it over to the mother at feeding time.

Many langurs have babies with bright orange fur (above). The adults are a grayish-brown color. Scientists think the color makes the babies attractive to the other langurs and helps keep them safe.

The white tuft on a baby gorilla's bottom shows up well in the dark.

I didn't know that

chimps use tools.

Chimpanzees are clever inventors. They have learned to peel long, thin twigs and then use them as fishing rods to "fish" out tasty termites from nests and mounds.

An ape's hand is like a human's. The thumb swivels around to touch each of the fingertips, allowing the owner to pick things up and handle them with care.

Chimpanzee

True or false?
Apes can learn a language.

Answer: **True**
Apes have intelligent minds. Over the years, scientists have studied the animals and have taught them to *communicate* with symbols and signs. One gorilla learned to "say" whole sentences in sign language. Other apes have learned more than 100 different symbols.

Monkeys learn from one another. It is said that in Japan, a young macaque found a potato on the beach and washed off the sand in the sea. Other macaques copied her and now they all wash their food.

Apes will never speak because they can't make the necessary sounds.

I didn't know that

eagles kill monkeys. Monkeys need to watch out for harpy eagles. These sharp-eyed hunters fly silently over the forest. They grab monkeys from the branches and crush them in their powerful claws.

Harpy eagle

Some monkeys have fangs.

Answer: **True**

Baboons have a pair of very long, pointed teeth (left). Males snarl and bare their fangs to frighten leopards, lions, and other hunters that threaten the group.

A male gorilla scares off its enemies by standing up tall, baring its teeth, roaring loudly, and beating its chest with its hands (right).

Capuchin monkey

I didn't know that

some gorillas have silver fur. Adult male gorillas are called silverbacks because the hair on their back turns silver-gray. A large silverback protects the troop and decides where it sleeps and feeds.

Mountain gorilla

SEARCH & FIND
Can you find the elephant?
FIND & SEARCH

24

Gorillas are the world's largest primates. They have massive skulls, sturdy legs, and powerful muscles. Yet, gorillas are gentle vegetarians. They eat shoots, roots, leaves, fruit, and fungi.

True or false?
Gorillas make nests in the trees.

Answer: **True**
Each evening, gorillas make nests of branches and leaves in the trees or on the ground. They make nests at midday, too, for a lunchtime nap.

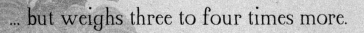
... but weighs three to four times more.

Apes and monkeys are so similar to humans that scientists use them for *research*. They test new *drugs* and have even sent chimps into space. Many people believe this is cruel and try to prevent it.

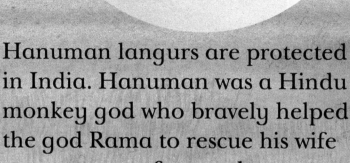

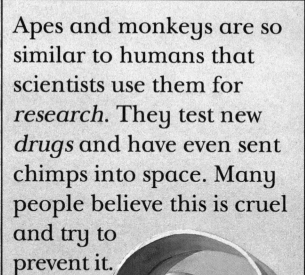

Hanuman langurs are protected in India. Hanuman was a Hindu monkey god who bravely helped the god Rama to rescue his wife from a demon.

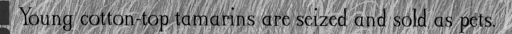

Young cotton-top tamarins are seized and sold as pets.

Zoos are breeding primates to return them to the wild.

SEARCH & FIND
Can you find the patrol jeep?
FIND & SEARCH &

I didn't know that

some monkeys and apes are orphans. When monkeys and apes are killed by hunters, their young become helpless orphans. Patrols take the babies to special parks, where they are brought up and protected.

Chimpanzee

The owl monkey lives in South America, and is the world's only *nocturnal* monkey. Its large eyes help it to see in the dark.

Owl monkey

The monkey with the longest nose is the male proboscis monkey from Southeast Asia. When he's excited, his nose turns red, which helps him to attract a mate.

The world's most famous primate appeared in the movie *King Kong*, made in the 1932 (left). The movie is about a giant gorilla and is set in New York City.

In ancient Egypt, Hamadryas baboons were sacred.

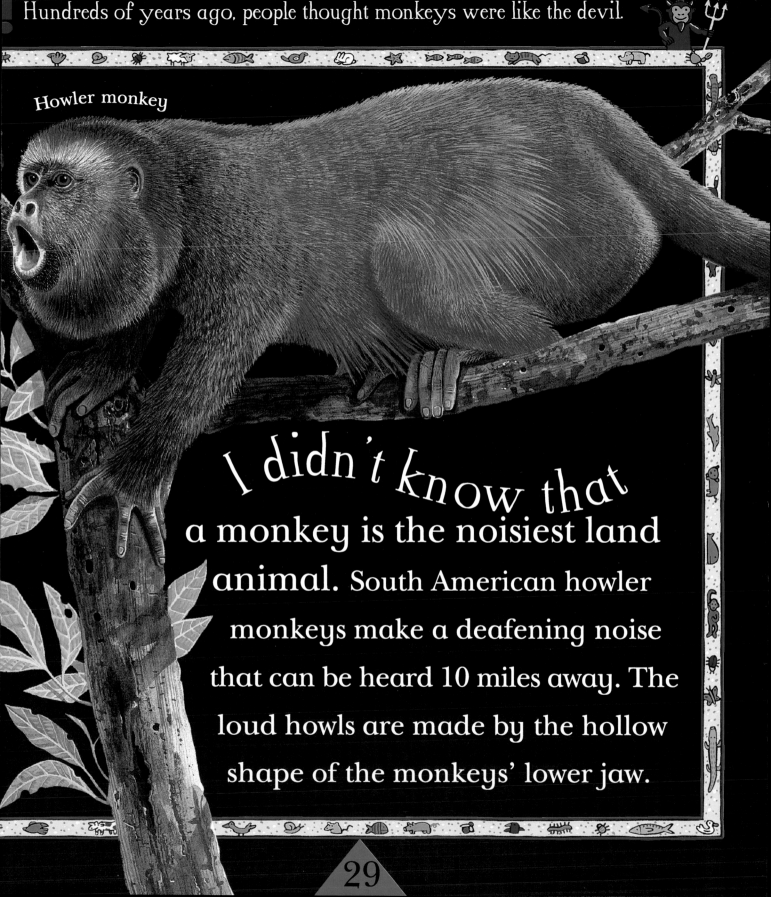

Howler monkey

I didn't know that a monkey is the noisiest land animal. South American howler monkeys make a deafening noise that can be heard 10 miles away. The loud howls are made by the hollow shape of the monkeys' lower jaw.

Glossary

Ancestor
A member of the same family that lived and died a long time ago.

Brachiating
Moving along by hanging from the branches and swinging one arm over the other.

Communicate
To share ideas, information, and feelings with another animal or person.

Drugs
Chemicals that work inside the body. Many drugs are medicines that fight disease.

Expression
A look on an animal's face that shows what it is feeling.

Fossil
Animal remains from millions of years ago that have turned to stone.

Nocturnal
Out and about at night.

Sap
A sweet liquid inside the stems and leaves of plants.

Sitting pads
The pads of hard skin on the bottom on which some apes and monkeys sit.

Prehensile
A part of an animal's body, such as a monkey's tail, that can curl around, seize, and hold onto things.

Primate
A member of the primate family, which includes humans, apes, and monkeys.

Research
To study something in order to discover some new information.

Index

ancestors 7, 30

babies 5, 14, 15, 18, 19, 27

baboons 5, 8, 14, 15, 23, 28

barbary apes 9

brachiating 12, 30

bushbabies 6

butterflies 13

capuchin monkeys 8, 22, 23

cheetahs 14

chimpanzees 10, 13, 15, 16, 18, 19, 20, 22, 26

communicating 21, 30

drugs 26, 30

expressions 16, 30

eyes 6, 22

fangs 5, 23

forests 8, 11, 12, 15, 17, 22

fossils 7, 30

gibbons 12, 15

gorillas 5, 7, 13, 19, 21, 23, 24, 25

grasslands 8, 14

grooming 14

Hanuman langurs 26

howler monkeys 29

intelligence 6, 20, 21

King Kong 28

knuckle-walking 13

langurs 19, 26

lemur 6

leopards 23

lions 14, 23

macaque 5, 9, 20, 21
  Japanese 9, 21
  pigtailed 20

nests 20, 25

nocturnal 28, 30

nostrils 8

orangutans 10, 15

orphans 27

owl monkeys 28

pigs 10

prehensile 11, 31

primates 6, 7, 18, 27, 31

proboscis monkeys 28

pythons 18

research 21, 31

Rock of Gibraltar 9

sap 10, 31

silverbacks 24

sitting pads 8, 16, 31

spider monkeys 11

squirrel monkeys 13

tamarins 26

tools 20

woolly monkeys 10, 11, 17

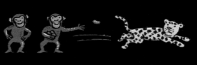

Titles available in the series:
I Didn't Know That

The **sun** is a star
You can jump higher on the **moon**
Some **snakes** spit poison
Some **bugs** glow in the dark
Spiders have fangs
Some **birds** hang upside down
Dinosaurs laid eggs
Some **trains** run on water
Some **planes** hover
Some **plants** grow in midair
Sharks keep losing their teeth
People chase **twisters**
Mountains gush lava and ash
Chimps use tools
Some **boats** have wings
Whales can sing
Only some **big cats** can roar
Crocodiles yawn to keep cool
Trucks and other construction machines
Quakes split the ground open